BRAIN-BUSTING PUZZLES

LOGIC

Sarah Khan

QEB Publishing

Editorial Director: Victoria Garrard
Art Director: Laura Roberts-Jensen
Designers: Austin Taylor and Rosie Levine
Illustrations by Julie Ingham

Copyright © QED Publishing 2014

First published in the UK in 2014 by
QED Publishing
A Quarto Group company
The Old Brewery
6 Blundell Street
London, N7 9BH

www.qed-publishing.co.uk

A catalogue record for this book is
available from the British Library.

ISBN 978 1 60992 627 4

Printed and bound in China

BB

Look out for the
puzzles marked as
Brain Busters—
they're the hardest!

Contents

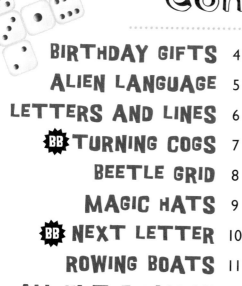

BIRTHDAY GIFTS

These birthday gifts have lost their tags. Who gave which gift? Use the clues below to find out.

- Sophie's gift had a black ribbon.
- Uncle Sam gave a cube-shaped gift.
- Amy's gift was wrapped in spotted paper.
- Grandma's gift was the smallest.
- Auntie Jo gave the tallest gift.

ALIEN LANGUAGE

In an alien language:

"Rqagof pri dai geva" means "We come in peace."

"Kerpi pri gad nist" means "We are your friends."

"Kerpi pri dai uda hoxi" means "We come to make friends."

Match the words to their meanings:

pri

we

come

friends

kerpi

dai

LETTERS AND LINES

Which of these diagrams is the odd one out?

TURNING COGS

UP

DOWN

Which way will you need to pull the lever on the top cog—up or down—to lift the weight?

BEETLE GRID

How many spots should the beetle in the blank square have?

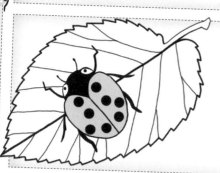
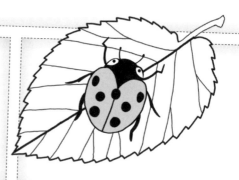

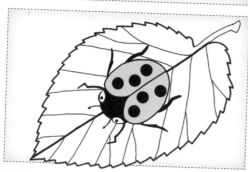
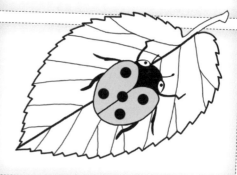

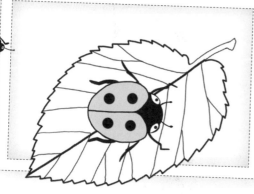
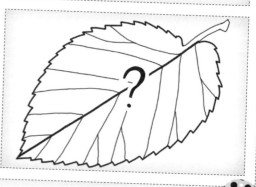

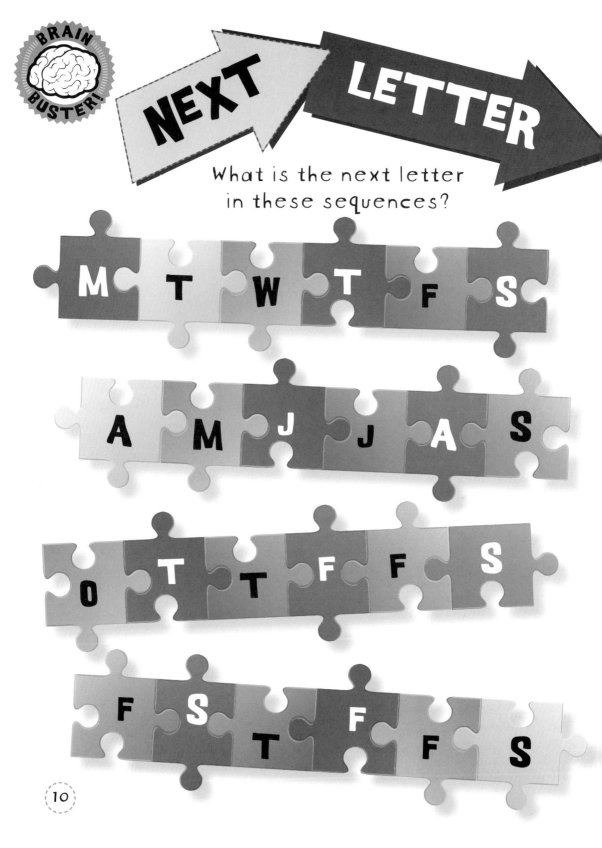

NEXT LETTER

BRAIN BUSTER!

What is the next letter in these sequences?

M T W T F S

A M J J A S

O T T F F S

F S T F F S

ROWING BOATS

A family visit a lake and want to go rowing. How many boats are there and how many people are in the family if the following statements are true?

If everyone wants to take a boat each, one person won't get a boat.

If the family go rowing in pairs, one boat will be left unused.

ALL IN THE FAMILY

1

Jason's parents have three children. Two of them are called April and May. What is their third child called?

2

Quentin's father is the brother of Preston and the son of Michael. Sonny is the son of Preston and the brother of Theo. How is Michael related to Theo?

3

Two daughters and two mothers go to a clothes shop. Each person buys one dress, but they only buy three dresses altogether. How is that possible?

On dice, the spots on each pair of opposite sides add up to 7. All of the shapes below can be folded up to make a cube, but which one will make a dice?

A

B

C

D

13

ROBOT FACTORY

At the robot factory, each type of robot has a manufacturing code. By looking at these robots and their codes, can you find out which of the robots below has the code QX?

Code: QZ

Code: KW

Code: RX

A

B

C

BROKEN WINDOW

Three boys were playing with a ball in the school playground when one of them accidentally smashed a classroom window. When they were called into the principal's office, they gave these statements:

ROBBIE: Jordan did it!
JORDAN: Sam did it!
SAM: Jordan is lying!

If two of them are telling the truth and one of them is lying, can you find out from their statements which of them smashed the window?

GROWING UP

Have a look at how zebra 1 changes as it grows from a baby to an adult. Which one of the zebras below will zebra 2 grow into?

CIRCLE NUMBERS

Place the numbers 0, 1, or 2 in the circles below to make each sentence true. You can only use each number once.

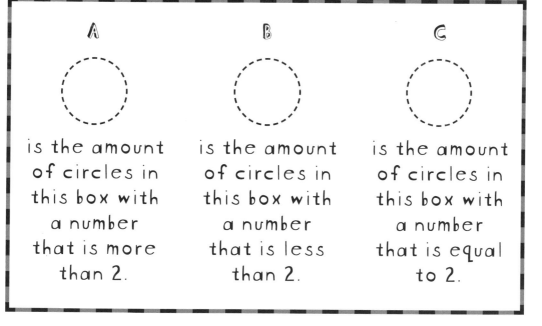

A is the amount of circles in this box with a number that is more than 2.

B is the amount of circles in this box with a number that is less than 2.

C is the amount of circles in this box with a number that is equal to 2.

Following the sequence, what comes next: A, B, or C

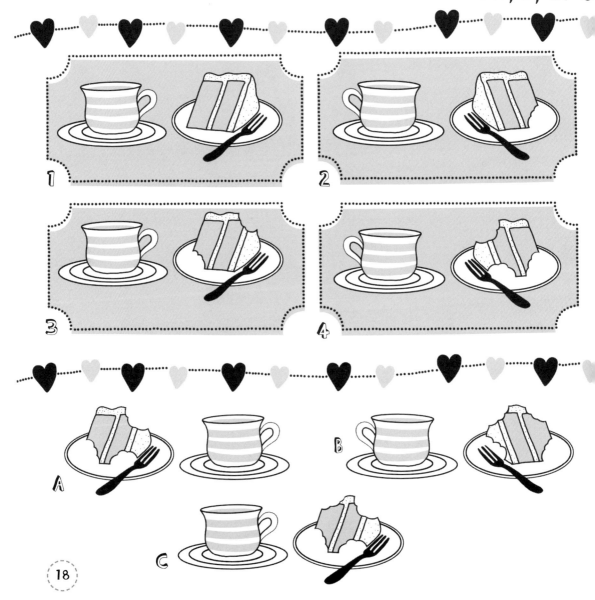

CHECKOUT CHALLENGE

1. Which item is three items to the right of the item that is directly right of the item that is three items to the left of the item that is directly right of the bananas?

2. Which item is four items to the left of the item that is directly right of the item that is two items to the right of the item that is directly left of the ketchup?

WORD SQUARES

In each set of four squares, find the relationship between the two words that are next to each other. Then, use that same relationship to find out what the missing word in the set should be. The first one has been completed for you.

dog — puppy
cat — kitten

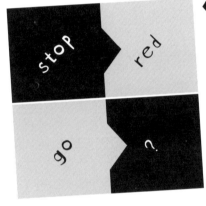

stop — red
go — ?

A

tricycle — ?
bicycle — two

B

? — desert
water — ocean

C

VENDING MACHINE

Two children go to a toy vending machine. If they put a coin in the machine, a toy will fall out. The machine contains three types of toy: dinosaurs, cars, and superheroes. The children don't mind what type of toy they get, as long as they both get the same one. What is the most amount of coins that they might have to spend to make sure that they both get the same type of toy?

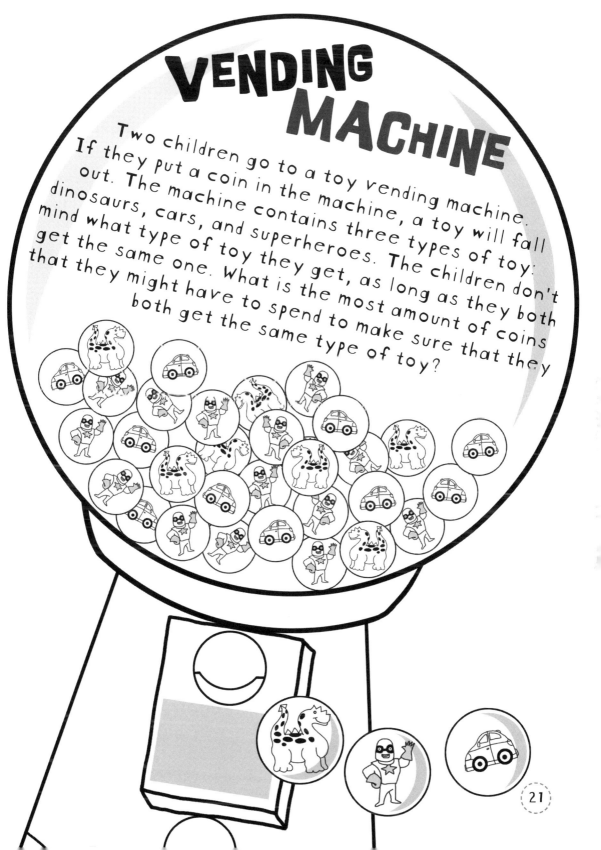

SACK RACE

Aaron, Billie, Chloe, Donna, and Emma took part in a sack race. Aaron finished before Billie but behind Chloe. Donna finished before Emma but behind Billie.

Put the children in order of the where they finished in the race, from first to last.

WEIGHING SCALES

How many triangles will you need to balance the third set of scales?

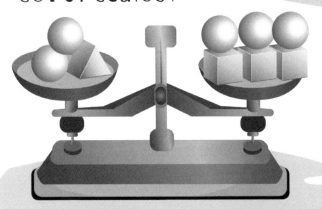

SOLID PROOF

In each set of statements, which two prove that:

1
Joe is eating chocolate cake.

A. Joe loves chocolate cake.
B. Joe's sister is eating chocolate cake.
C. Chocolate cake is the only cake in Joe's house.
D. Joe is eating the same cake as his sister.
E. Joe's sister has made some chocolate cake.

2
Mia won a relay race.

A. Mia ran in the same relay race team as Kate.
B. Mia is the fastest runner on her team.
C. Mia's team was very happy after the relay race.
D. Kate and Mia train very hard.
E. Kate's team came first in the relay race.

3
Paul is a DJ on the radio.

A. Paul listens to the radio every day.
B. Paul plays a lot of music.
C. Paul works at a radio station in the afternoons.
D. Paul talks a lot at work.
E. Paul spends his afternoons playing music.

FOUR SQUARE

How can you fill the grid below so that the numbers 1, 2, 3 and 4 appear once in every line, column and block of four squares?

COUNTING CUBES

How many cubes
are there in each
of these solid
structures?

A

B

LONG LINE

Ada, Bob, and Cedric are standing in a line. There are five people between Ada and Bob and eight people between Bob and Cedric. Cedric is ahead of Bob and Ada is behind Bob. If there are only 3 people ahead of Cedric and 21 people behind Ada, how many people are there in the line?

LETTER CODE

Secret Agent 770 has received a coded message from Headquarters letting him know where he should meet Agent 880 in Egypt. He has decoded one of the words in the message. Can you decode the others?

BRAIN BUSTER!

PHHW WKH DJHQW DW
WKH SBUDPLGV QHAW
WR WKH FDPHO ULGHUV

AGENT

ODD ONES OUT

Which is the odd one out in each line?

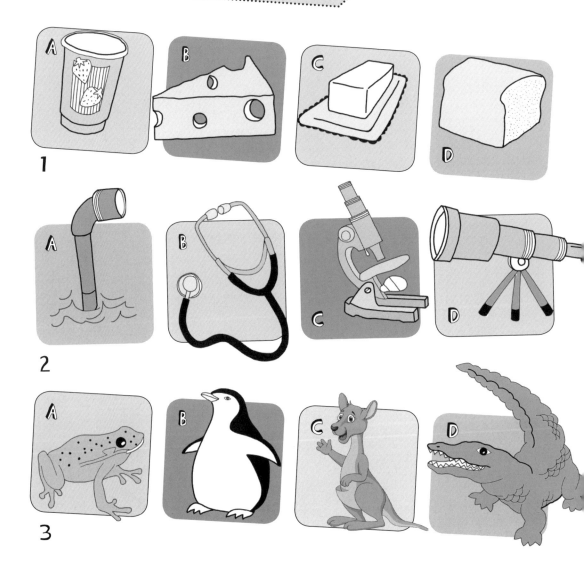

1

2

3

REFLECTIONS

The reflections of these statues have become mixed up in the water below. Match the statues to their reflections.

TALL AND SHORT

There are five friends: Simon, Katie, Mo, Anna, and Rhea. Simon is shorter than Katie but taller than Rhea. Mo is tallest. Anna is a little shorter than Katie and a little taller than Simon.

Put the friends in order of height, starting from the tallest.

Which of the flags below should come next in the sequence?

FLAG SEQUENCE

A

B

C

D

SPINNING AROUND

A

All but one of these figures can be spun around to match each other. Which is the odd one out?

D

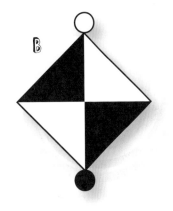

B

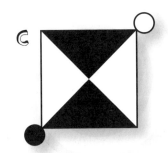

C

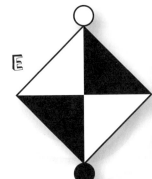

E

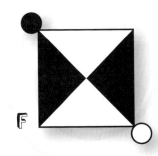

F

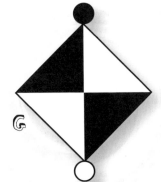

G

THE RIGHT DIRECTION

A mouse runs 20 steps toward East and turns right, runs 10 steps and turns right again. Then, it runs 9 steps and turns left, runs 5 steps and then turns left again and runs 12 steps. Finally the mouse turns left and runs 6 steps. Now in which direction is the mouse facing?

JUMBLED UP

These instructions on how to draw a boat have become jumbled up. What is the right order?

A

C

B

E

D

F

G

PLAYING CARDS

There are three playing cards held up below. Use these clues to find out which card is which.

B A C

- A club is somewhere to the left of a diamond.

Q2

- A 2 is directly to the right of a queen.

9♥

- A 9 is directly to the left of a heart.

- A heart is directly to the left of a diamond.

WHAT AM I?

1 I am weightless, but you can see me. Put me in a bucket, and I'll make it lighter. What am I?

2 I'm light as a feather, yet the strongest man can't hold me for much more than a minute. What am I?

3

4 I have four legs, one head and a foot. What am I?

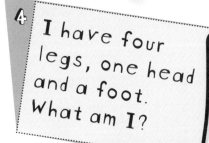

5 Many have heard me, but none have seen me. I will not answer unless spoken to. What am I?

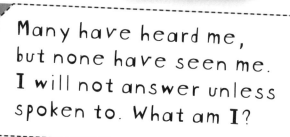

IN COMMON

In each group, the top two figures have something in common with each other. They have that same thing in common with one of the other figures beneath them. Which one?

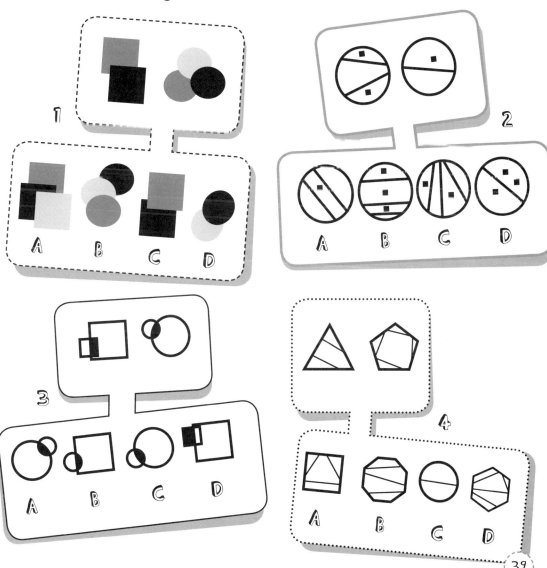

1

A B C D

2

A B C D

3

A B C D

4

A B C D

JOINING PATTERNS

Which of the patterns below is made when these two patterns are put together then spun around?

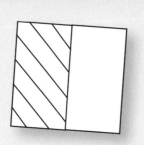 **+**   **=**

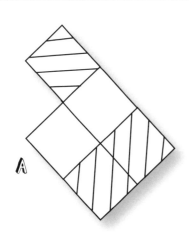

A

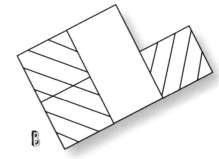

B

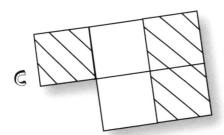

C

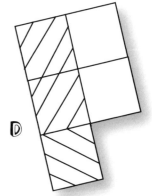

D

PET PUZZLE

Molly, Suzie, Tom, and Dan each have a different kind of pet. Look at the pictures of their pets and use these clues to find out which pet belongs to which child:

Tom's pet sleeps all winter.

Molly's pet has fur.

Dan's pet drinks milk.

SHELL COLLECTORS

The Smith family are collecting shells on the beach. Use these clues to find out how many shells the whole family has collected:

Mrs. Smith has 2 fewer shells than her daughter, Emma.

Mr. Smith has 1 more shell than his wife.

Emma has 6 cockle shells and 4 mussel shells in total.

Luke has half the number of shells that Emma has.

COUNTING THE DAYS

Alia has a busy month planned. She has circled the important dates on her calendar. Look at the circled days and use the clues below to find out the date of each of her activities.

She is volunteering at an animal shelter on a weekend.

She is singing in a concert some time in this month.

She is going bowling two weeks before the sleepover.

She is going to her friend's sleepover on a Saturday night.

She has her first karate lesson on the fourth week of the month.

LINK WORDS

Which of the words from each list links the images on either side of them?

A

animal
glass
pet
black
sun

B

man
food
cold
winter
cone

C

leaves
float
green
row
wood

TURNING CUBE

If each side of the cube on the right is different, which one of the cubes below shows this cube turned on its side?

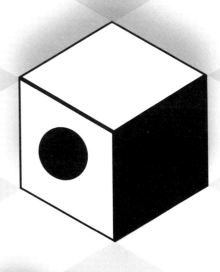

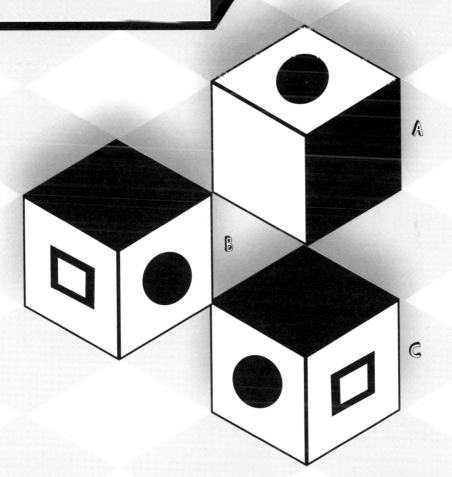

A

B

C

PATTERN MACHINE

When you put a shape into the pattern machine, it makes it into a pattern. Look at what the machine has done to the triangle. If it does exactly the same thing to the rectangle, which of the patterns below will it make?

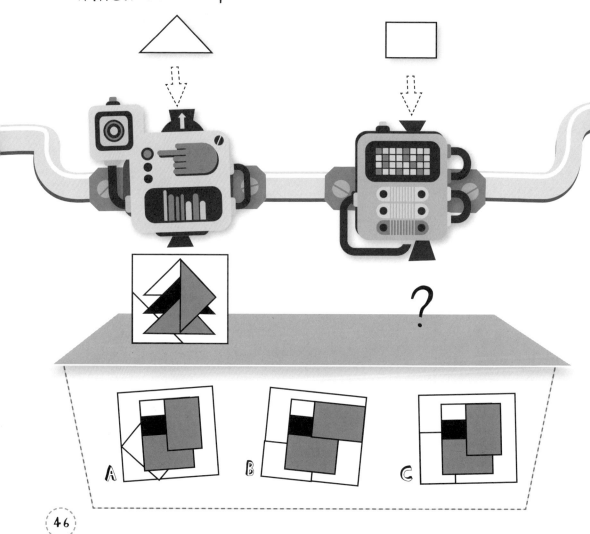

A

B

C

MURDER MYSTERY

Four friends are watching a murder mystery set in an old English country mansion.

Ali thinks that the victim's wife killed him.

Kim is certain the butler is the murderer.

Sean is sure that the maid is the culprit.

Pat thinks that either the maid or the wife is the killer.

If only one of the friends is right, which character is the murderer?

Answers

page 4:
A. Uncle Sam
B. Amy
C. Ben & Holly
D. Auntie Jo
E. Grandma
F. Sophie
page 5: "pri" means "we"
"kerpi" means "friends"
"dai" means "come"
page 6:

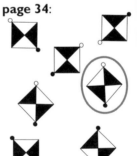

(The two As aren't connected.)
page 7: Down
page 8: 3
The beetles in the left column have an even number of spots descending from 8 to 4, and the right column has odd numbers from 7 to 3.
page 9:
Hat A contains the rabbit.
Hat B contains the flowers.
Hat C contains the dove.
page 10:
1. S (for Sunday)
2. O (for October)
3. S (for seven)
4. S (for seventh)
page 11: There are four people in the family and three boats.
page 12:
1. Jason
2. Michael is Theo's grandfather.
3. There were only three women—one was both a mother and a daughter.

page 13: C
page 14: B
The first letter refers to the robot's head and the second to its body.
page 15: Jordan
page 16: A (There are twice the amount of lines on the adult zebra's body than on the baby zebra's body.)
page 17: A.0, B.2, C.1
page 18: C
page 19: 1. Mustard
2. Cereal
page 20: A. green,
B. three, C. sand
page 21: 4 (If they spend 3 coins, they might get 3 different toys, but the 4th coin will get them one of the toys they already have.)
page 22: 1. Chloe,
2. Aaron, 3. Billie,
4. Donna, 5. Emma
page 23: A and D
page 24: 2 (1 triangle = 2 circles, 1 circle = 3 squares)
page 25: 1. B and D, 2. A and E, 3. C and E
page 26:

2	4	1	3
3	1	4	2
1	3	2	4
4	2	3	1

page 27: A. 8, B. 15
page 28: 40
page 29: MEET THE AGENT AT THE PYRAMIDS NEXT TO THE CAMEL RIDERS.
Each letter has moved three steps forward in the alphabet to make the code.

page 30: 1. D (Bread is made from wheat, while the others are all milk products.)
2. B (The stethoscope is used for hearing things, while the others are used for looking at things.)
3. C (A kangaroo gives birth to live young, while the others all lay eggs OR the other animals live in and around water.)
page 31:
1. C, 2. A, 3. D, 4. B
page 32: Mo, Katie, Anna, Simon, Rhea
page 33: D
The cross moves from left to right and the star and wheel move in a clockwise direction.
page 34:

page 35: North
page 36: F, A, G, D, C, B, E
page 37:

page 38:
1. A hole
2. Breath
3. Your name
4. A bed
5. An echo
page 39:
1. D (The black shape should be at the front.)
2. B (There should be the same number of squares as there are lines inside each circle.)
3. C (The small shape should be the same as the big shape, on the left side of the big shape and should have the overlapping part shaded black.)
4. A (There should be one less line inside the shape than the number of sides of the shape.)
page 40: A
page 41: Molly's pet is the guinea pig.
Suzie's pet is the budgie.
Tom's pet is the tortoise.
Dan's pet is the kitten.
page 42: 32
Emma has 10 shells.
Mrs. Smith has 8 shells.
Mr. Smith has 9 shells.
Luke has 5 shells.
page 43:
She is going:
• singing on Tuesday 3rd
• bowling on Saturday 14th
• volunteering on Sunday 15th
• to karate on Wednesday 25th
• to the sleepover on Saturday 28th
page 44: A. black, B. cold, C. wood
page 45: C
page 46: A
page 47: the butler